D0421754

Other Helen Exley Giftbooks

...And Wisdom Comes Quietly
Words on Hope
In Times of Trouble
Words on Compassion
Your Journey
Words of Comfort

Published simultaneously in 2003 by Exley Publications Ltd
in Great Britain, and Exley Publications LLC in the USA.

2 4 6 8 10 12 11 9 7 5 3 1

ISBN 1-86187-543-6

Edited by Helen Exley.
Illustrated by Juliette Clarke.
Printed in China.

Exley Publications Ltd,
16 Chalk Hill, Watford, Herts WD19 4BG, UK

Exley Publications LLC,
185 Main Street, Spencer, MA 01562, USA

www.helenexleygiftbooks.com

Bulk copies of this book are available at special discounts for promotional purposes,
and for charity fundraising. Please contact *Dept P. Special Sales* for details.

A SPECIAL GIFT OF
HOPE & COURAGE

Illustrated by Juliette Clarke
A HELEN EXLEY GIFTBOOK

LIVE BRAVE!

*...I'm not going to lie down
and let trouble walk over me.*

ELLEN GLASGOW (1874-1945)

*There are really only two ways
to approach life: as victim or
as gallant fighter. You must decide
if you want to act or react.
And if you don't decide which way to play
with life, it always plays with you.*

MERLE SHAIN

There's something so vibrant and gutsy
about courage; just do it.

ANITA RODDICK, B.1943, FROM "VOICES FROM THE HEART"

If I were asked to give what I consider
the single most useful bit of advice
for all humanity it would be this:
Expect trouble as an inevitable part of life
and when it comes, hold your head high,
look it squarely in the eye and say,
"I will be bigger than you.
You cannot defeat me."

ANN LANDERS, B.1918

WHEN YOUR BOW IS BROKEN AND YOUR
LAST ARROW SPENT, THEN SHOOT,
SHOOT WITH YOUR WHOLE HEART.

ZEN SAYING

THE PATHWAY
THROUGH TROUBLES

*Obstacles in the pathway of the weak
become stepping stones in the pathway
of the strong.*

THOMAS CARLYLE (1795-1881)

Every problem has a gift
for you in its hands.

RICHARD BACH

*Grant that I may be given appropriate
difficulties and sufferings on this journey
so that my heart might be truly awakened
and my practice of liberation
and compassion may be truly fulfilled.*

TIBETAN PRAYER

*The marvelous richness of human
experience would lose something of rewarding
joy if there were not limitations to overcome.
The hilltop hour would not be
half so wonderful if there
were no dark valleys to traverse.*

HELEN KELLER (1880-1968)

REAL HEROISM

THE COURAGE OF VERY ORDINARY PEOPLE IS
ALL THAT STANDS BETWEEN US AND THE DARK.

PAM BROWN, B.1928

Disasters sweep the world – war and disease,
earthquake and flood and fire – but always
in their wake come acts of courage
and concern that astound the human heart.
Light in utter darkness.

CHARLOTTE GRAY, B.1937

Heroism is the brilliant triumph
over fear.... Heroism is the dazzling
and brilliant concentration of courage.

HENRI FRÉDÉRIC AMIEL (1821-1881)

The generations ask "Has life a meaning?"
But those who have courage act
as if each life had purpose and so give this
planet a dignity beyond all reason.

PAM BROWN, B.1928

SURVIVAL

*I was always looking outside myself
for strength and confidence but it comes
from within. It is there all the time.*

ANNA FREUD (1895-1982)

*We attempt nothing great but from a sense
of the difficulties we encounter;
we persevere in nothing great but
from a pride in overcoming them.*

WILLIAM HAZLITT (1778-1830)

*I'm a survivor. Being a survivor
doesn't mean you have to be made out
of steel. It means you are basically on your
own side and you want to win.*

LINDA RONSTADT

HOPE

THE DEEPEST PRISON,
SEALED OFF FROM LIGHT AND SOUND,
CANNOT HOLD THE HUMAN SPIRIT
IF HOPE ENDURES. IT IS
A WINDOW TO THE WIDER WORLD.
IT IS THE LINK TO LOVE.

PAM BROWN, B.1928

Despite the sight of all the miseries which
affect us and hold us by the throat we have
an irrepressible instinct which bears us up.

BLAISE PASCAL (1623-1662)

When we are flat on our backs
there is no way to look but up.

ROGER W. BABSON

*Hope is a very quiet thing,
but strong. With little sustenance, it can
endure. With little light it can survive.
It makes life possible.*

CHARLOTTE GRAY, B.1937

The important thing is not that we can
live on hope alone, but that
life is not worth living without it.

HARVEY MILK

NEVER FORGET HAPPINESS

I don't think of all the misery but
of the beauty that still remains.

ANNE FRANK (1929-1945)

Courage... is nothing less than
the power to overcome danger, misfortune,
fear, injustice, while continuing to affirm
inwardly that life, with all its sorrows,
is good; that everything is meaningful,
even if in a sense beyond our understanding;
and that there is always tomorrow.

DOROTHY THOMPSON (1894-1961)

EVEN IF HAPPINESS FORGETS YOU
A LITTLE BIT, NEVER COMPLETELY FORGET
ABOUT IT.

JACQUES PRÉVERT (1900-1977)

In spite of all,
some shape of beauty moves away
the pall from our dark spirits.

JOHN KEATS (1795-1821)

TRUE COURAGE

Courage is never letting your actions
be influenced by your fears.

ARTHUR KOESTLER (1905-1983)

Grant me the courage
not to give up,
even though I think
it is hopeless.

CHESTER W. NIMITZ (1885-1966)

To keep our faces toward
change and behave like
free spirits in the presence of fate
is strength undefeatable.

HELEN KELLER (1880-1968)

The great virtue in life
is real courage
that knows how to face facts
and live beyond them.

D.H. LAWRENCE (1885-1930)

WEALTH LOST – SOMETHING LOST;
HONOR LOST – MUCH LOST;
COURAGE LOST – ALL LOST.

OLD GERMAN PROVERB

ONE OF THE FINEST QUALITIES
IS DESCRIBED BY
THE SIMPLE WORD "GUTS"
– THE ABILITY TO TAKE IT.
IF YOU HAVE THE DISCIPLINE
TO STAND FAST
WHEN YOUR BODY WANTS TO RUN,
IF YOU CAN CONTROL
YOUR TEMPER AND REMAIN
CHEERFUL IN THE FACE OF
MONOTONY OR DISAPPOINTMENT,
YOU HAVE "GUTS".

JOHN S. ROOSMAN

Look well into yourself;
there is a source of strength
which will always spring up if you
always look there.

MARCUS AURELIUS (121-80 B.C.)

SPEAK OUT FOR WHAT YOU BELIEVE

Moral cowardice that keeps us from
speaking our minds is as dangerous
as irresponsible talk. The right way
is not always the popular and easy way.
Standing for right when it is unpopular
is a true test of moral character.

MARGARET CHASE SMITH

The frontiers are not east or west, north or
south, but wherever someone fronts a fact.

HENRY DAVID THOREAU (1817-1862)

*From the cowardice that shrinks from
new truth, from the laziness that
is content with half-truths, deliver us.*

ANCIENT PRAYER

YOUR COURAGE MAY WELL
LIFT THE HEARTS
OF A THOUSAND — AND HELP THEM
TO MOVE FORWARD.

PAM BROWN, B.1928

*The ability to pursue a course,
whether it is a popular one or not,
is measured in courage. The greater
the courage, the greater the possibility
we will act for change.*

MILDRED PITTS WALTER,
FROM "THE HORN BOOK"

LOVE COMMANDS US

*Love commands us
to step out into
nothingness – and
bears us up.*

PAM BROWN, B.1928

ONLY THE
LOVING ARE COURAGEOUS...

LAO-TZU
(6TH CENTURY B.C.)

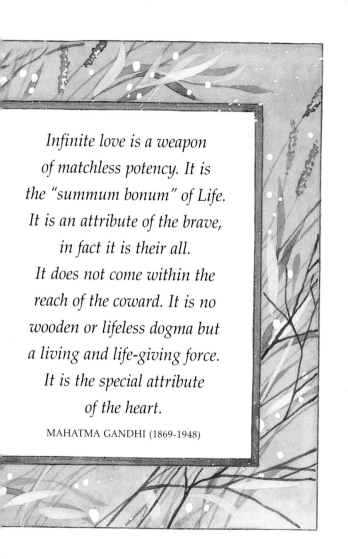

*Infinite love is a weapon
of matchless potency. It is
the "summum bonum" of Life.
It is an attribute of the brave,
in fact it is their all.
It does not come within the
reach of the coward. It is no
wooden or lifeless dogma but
a living and life-giving force.
It is the special attribute
of the heart.*

MAHATMA GANDHI (1869-1948)

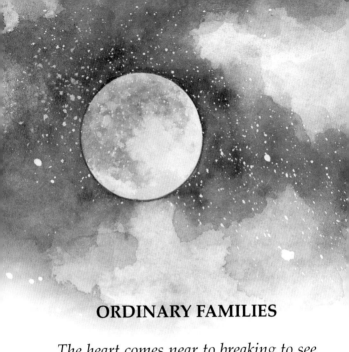

ORDINARY FAMILIES

*The heart comes near to breaking to see
ordinary families attempt to escape to freedom
– to face great danger to find a better life.
Only to be turned back to hunger, poverty,
disease, homes destroyed, livelihoods lost.
Courage beyond our understanding.
Grief beyond our experience.*

There is a courage we can scarcely
comprehend – the courage of people
driven to the very edges of existence.
Each day can bring the victory of survival –
or a heartbreaking defeat.
Each day carries the fear of loss,
and a struggle to keep hope alive.
And yet they endure.
And sing their songs.
And cherish hope for their children.

...

TO LIVE IN UTTER POVERTY, TO CREATE

MEALS FROM ALMOST NOTHING, TO KEEP

THE CHILDREN CLOTHED AND SAFE,

TO BRING LAUGHTER INTO DREARINESS.

– THIS IS TRUE, ENDURING COURAGE.

PAM BROWN, B.1928

STRENGTH

*You gain strength, courage,
and confidence by every experience
in which you really stop to look fear
in the face. You are able to say to yourself,
"I lived through this horror. I can take
the next thing that comes along."*

ELEANOR ROOSEVELT (1884-1962)

IT IS RIGHT TO BE AFRAID — FEAR IS
OUR WARNING AND PROTECTOR.
BUT TO FACE FEAR WITH COURAGE
AND INTELLIGENCE, PURPOSE
AND CHEERFULNESS, IS TO DEFEAT ALL
DANGER, IS TO GROW IN STATURE, IS TO
KEEP ALIVE THE HOPES OF US ALL.

PAM BROWN, B.1928

DETERMINATION

What one has to do usually can be done.

ELEANOR ROOSEVELT (1884-1962)

Time and I against any two.

SPANISH PROVERB

STAND THROUGH LIFE FIRM
AS A ROCK IN THE SEA,
UNDISTURBED AND UNMOVED
BY ITS EVER-RISING WAVES.

HAZRAT INAYAT KHAN (1882-1927)

Tough times don't last – tough people do.

AUTHOR UNKNOWN

Never give in. Never. Never. Never. Never.

SIR WINSTON CHURCHILL (1874-1965)

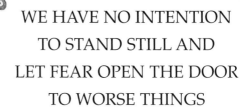

WE HAVE NO INTENTION
TO STAND STILL AND
LET FEAR OPEN THE DOOR
TO WORSE THINGS

Near is the lion on our path. But if we turn around and face it straight-on, it will slink away. The sooner we learn that fear has no power but what we give it, the sooner we gain control of all our emotions. The Tsalagi may know fear, but his stoic expression will never reveal it. To a Cherokee, u na ye hi s di, fear or alarm,

is the face of the enemy that tries
to numb his mind and spirit to make
it easier to conquer him. The lion's
roar is silenced the minute we face it
down with our own ga na nv di s gi,
war whoop, that shows we mean
business. We have no intention to
stand still and let fear open the door
to worse things. By the faith words
of our mouths we turn away, not only
the lion, but all it represents.
I turn with a shout that we are saved!

LUTHER STANDING BEAR (1868-1939)

Our way is not soft grass,
it's a mountain path with lots of rocks.
But it goes upwards,
forward, toward the sun.

RUTH WESTHEIMER, B.1928

WE MUST PRESS ON

I avoid looking forward or backward,
and try to keep looking upward.

CHARLOTTE BRONTË (1816-1855)

WE MUST PRESS ON,
WHETHER WE WILL OR NO,
AND WE SHALL WALK
BETTER WITH OUR EYES BEFORE
US THAN WITH THEM
EVER CAST BEHIND.

JEROME K. JEROME (1859-1927)

You have to accept whatever comes and
the only important thing is that you meet it
with courage and the best you have to give.

ELEANOR ROOSEVELT (1884-1962)

FACING YOUR FEAR

...May fearlessness guard us behind and before!
May fearlessness surround us
above and below!
May we be without fear of friend and foe!
May we be without fear of the known
and the unknown!
May we be without fear by night and by day!
Let all the world be my friend!

TRANSLATED BY RAIMUNDO PANNIKER,
FROM "THE VEDAS"

Courage is resistance to fear,
mastery of fear, not absence of fear.

MARK TWAIN (1835-1910)

Bravery does not mean
you are without fear.
It means you have the courage
to face your fear.

RAMA VERNON, FROM "A LEAP OF FAITH"

I learned that courage was not the absence
of fear, but the triumph over it. I felt fear
myself more times than I can remember,
but I hid it behind a mask of boldness.
The brave man is not he who does not feel
afraid, but he who conquers that fear.

NELSON MANDELA, B.1918,
FROM "LONG WALK TO FREEDOM"

ACT FOR CHANGE

True morality consists not in following the beaten track, but in finding out the true path for ourselves and fearlessly following it.

MAHATMA GANDHI (1869-1948)

All you have to do is look straight and see the road, and when you see it, don't sit looking at it – walk.

AYN RAND (1905-1982)

One does what one must – in spite of personal consequences, in spite of obstacles and dangers and pressures – and that is the basis of all morality.

JOHN F. KENNEDY (1917-1963)

THE TIME WHEN YOU NEED TO DO
SOMETHING IS WHEN NO ONE ELSE
IS WILLING TO DO IT, WHEN PEOPLE
ARE SAYING IT CAN'T BE DONE.

MARY FRANCES BERRY, B.1938

I am only one; but still I am one.
I cannot do everything,
but still I can do something.

HELEN KELLER (1880-1968)

May you always find the courage to
stand against evil, whatever its disguise.

PAM BROWN, B.1928

If you think you're too small
to have an impact,
try going to bed with a mosquito.

ANITA RODDICK, B.1943

GROWING IN STRENGTH

WALLS HAVE BEEN BUILT
AGAINST US, BUT WE ARE
FIGHTING TO TEAR THEM DOWN,
AND IN THE FIGHTING,
WE GROW, WE FIND NEW STRENGTH,
NEW SCOPE.

ESLANDA GODE ROBESON

*We ought to remember that we
are not the only ones to find ourselves
at an apparent impasse. Just as a kite
rises against the wind, even the worst
of troubles can strengthen us.
As thousands before us have met the
identical fate and mastered it, so can we!*

DR. R. BRASCH

I DO NOT ASK TO WALK
SMOOTH PATHS,
NOR BEAR AN EASY LOAD.
GIVE ME COURAGE TO SCALE
THE HARDEST PEAKS ALONE,
AND TRANSFORM EVERY
STUMBLING BLOCK
INTO A STEPPING STONE.

GAIL BROOK BURKETT

COURAGE LOOKS
YOU STRAIGHT IN THE EYE

Courage looks you straight
in the eye. She is not impressed
with power trippers, and she knows
first aid. Courage is not afraid
to weep, and she is not afraid to pray,
even when she is not sure
who she is praying to. When she walks
it is clear she has made the journey
from loneliness to solitude.
The people who told me
she was stern were not lying;
they just forgot to mention
she was kind.

J. RUTH GENDLER

BRAVE FAMILIES

*A moment of courage in the heat of battle
is courage enough – but the long-enduring
courage of the man or woman, or the child,
who, victims of persecution or catastrophe,
struggle to hold their family together,
to find food and shelter,
to hold out hope when hope is gone.
These are the true,
unlauded, heroes and heroines.*

...

*Most ordinary people astound the world
by their courage in adversity.
They matter more than kings or states
or creeds. In them, the world endures.*

...

No-one who has not dealt
with terror and loss and lack
of hope can begin to visualize
the courage of those attempting
to escape from persecution
and make a good life for
themselves and all they love.

PAM BROWN, B.1928

WE EACH HAVE OUR
SECRET COURAGE

We each have our secret fears.
We each have our secret courage.

...

There are many of us who are born
without courage – and yet we
endure, holding on by our
fingertips, against all odds.

...

We are astonished by
our capacity for courage –
human beings are far more brave
than they ever suspect possible.

...

IT IS VERY HARD
TO LIVE OUT A LIFE OF QUIET,
HIDDEN COURAGE.
IT IS FAR HARDER TO ENDURE IT
WITHOUT ACKNOWLEDGEMENT.
HOLD ON.
YOU ARE THE THREAD
THAT HOLDS
THE WORLD TOGETHER.

PAM BROWN, B.1928

A CERTAIN KIND OF COURAGE

*There is the courage that blazes
in a sudden rush of adrenalin – the courage
that achieves outrageous feats of daring.
And there is the courage that is built
from fear and hesitation, on long endurance
and quiet determination. The courage
that weighs the odds – and still
goes forward. The courage that faces pain
and near-despair with a hopeful heart –
and lifts the spirits of all around.
The desolate, the very old, the very young –
those facing unknown terrors....
They have no accolades. Only respect
and awe and gratitude. Only love.*

PAM BROWN, B.1928

THE BRAVEST ARE THOSE WHO ARE MOST AFRAID, BUT THAT ENDURE.

PAM BROWN, B.1928

To endure is greater than to dare; to tire out hostile fortune; to be daunted by no difficulty; to keep heart when all have lost it – who can say this is not greatness?

WILLIAM MAKEPEACE THACKERAY (1811-1863)

The only courage that matters is the kind that gets you from one moment to the next.

MIGNON MCLAUGHLIN

As time went on my thoughtless optimism
was transmuted into that deeper faith
that weighs the ugly facts of the world,
yet hopes for better things and keeps on
working for them even in the face of defeat.

HELEN KELLER (1880-1968)

COURAGE – A PERFECT
SENSIBILITY OF THE MEASURE
OF DANGER,
AND A MENTAL WILLINGNESS
TO ENDURE IT.

WILLIAM T. SHERMAN (1820-1891)

KEEP ON – KEEP ON GOING

You gotta stick it out, because there's only one ball-game here, and it's your own life. You got no choice. You got to play to win if you want to stay on this earth.

ADVICE GIVEN TO CANCER PATIENT JAMES BROWN

WHEN YOU GET INTO
A TIGHT PLACE AND EVERYTHING
GOES AGAINST YOU,
TILL IT SEEMS AS THOUGH
YOU COULD NOT HOLD ON
A MINUTE LONGER,
NEVER GIVE UP THEN, FOR THAT
IS JUST THE PLACE AND TIME
THAT THE TIDE WILL TURN.

HARRIET BEECHER STOWE (1811-1896)

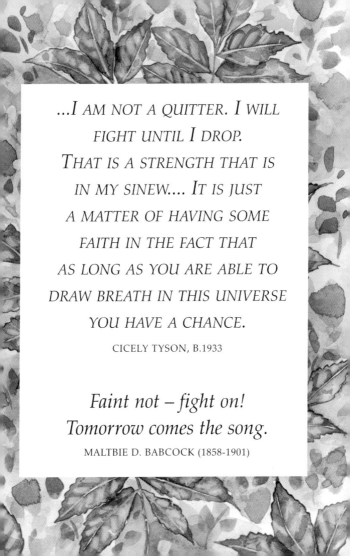

*...I AM NOT A QUITTER. I WILL
FIGHT UNTIL I DROP.
THAT IS A STRENGTH THAT IS
IN MY SINEW.... IT IS JUST
A MATTER OF HAVING SOME
FAITH IN THE FACT THAT
AS LONG AS YOU ARE ABLE TO
DRAW BREATH IN THIS UNIVERSE
YOU HAVE A CHANCE.*

CICELY TYSON, B.1933

*Faint not – fight on!
Tomorrow comes the song.*

MALTBIE D. BABCOCK (1858-1901)

TOMORROW WILL BE
THE BEGINNING...

There is a feeling of absolute finality
about the end of a flight through darkness.
The whole scheme of things with which
you have lived acutely, during hours
of roaring sound in an element altogether
detached from the world, ceases abruptly....
The dream of flight is suddenly gone
before the mundane realities of growing grass
and swirling dust, the slow plodding of men
and the enduring patience of rooted trees.

BERYL MARKHAM

...misfortune and destruction are not final.
When the grass has been burnt by the fire
of the steppe, it will grow anew in summer.

MONGOLIAN WISDOM

GENTLENESS AND LOVE
WILL RETURN

*Though no one can go back
and make a new start, anyone
can start from now and make
a brand new end.*

CARL BARD

*Under the storm
and the cloud today, and today
the hard peril and pain
— tomorrow the stone
shall be rolled away,
for the sunshine
shall follow the rain.*

JOAQUIN MILLER (1839-1913)

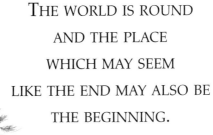

THE WORLD IS ROUND
AND THE PLACE
WHICH MAY SEEM
LIKE THE END MAY ALSO BE
THE BEGINNING.

IVY BAKER PRIEST (1905-1975)

What is a *Helen Exley Giftbook*?

Helen Exley has been creating giftbooks for twenty-seven years, and her readers have bought forty-eight million copies of her works in over thirty languages. Because her books are all bought as gifts, she spares no expense in making sure that each book is as thoughtful and meaningful a gift as it is possible to create: good to give, good to receive. Hope and courage in times of trouble are concerns that are very central to Helen's work and she has created several titles on these themes.

Team members help to find thoughtful quotations from literally hundreds of sources, and the books are then personally created. With infinite care, Helen Exley ensures that each illustration matches each quotation, that each spread is individually designed to enhance the feeling of the words, and that the whole book has real depth and meaning.

You have the result in your hands. If you have loved it – tell others! There is no power on earth like the word-of-mouth recommendation of friends.

Helen Exley Giftbooks
16 Chalk Hill, Watford, Herts WD19 4BG, UK
185 Main Street, Spencer, MA 01562, USA
www.helenexleygiftbooks.com

Acknowledgements: The publishers are grateful for permission to reproduce copyright material. Whilst every reasonable effort has been made to trace copyright holders, we would be pleased to hear from any not here acknowledged. LUTHER STANDING BEAR: From *Land of the Spotted Eagle*, published by the University of Nebraska Press. Published with permission. J. RUTH GENDLER: "Courage" from *The Book of Qualities*, HarperCollins, © 1988 by J. Ruth Gendler. Reprinted with permission of the author. BERYL MARKHAM: From *West with the Night* by Beryl Markham, published by North Point Press. Used by permission of Pollinger Ltd. PAM BROWN, CHARLOTTE GRAY: published with permission © Helen Exley 2003.

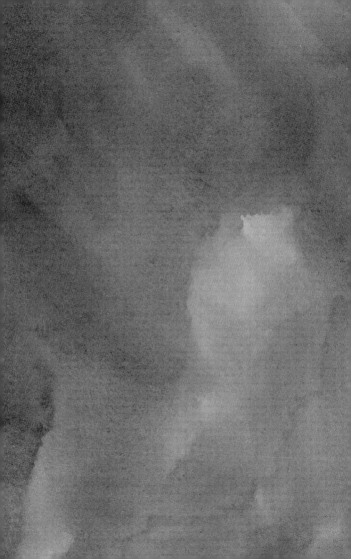